□ FIGHTING FOR THEIR FAITH □

St. Francis of Assisi renounced his worldly goods to lead a simple life as a preacher and a pilgrim.

TALES OF COURAGE

◻

FIGHTING FOR THEIR FAITH

◻

BY BRENDA CLARKE

Illustrated by Andrew Howat

◻

STECK-VAUGHN
L I B R A R Y
A Division of Steck-Vaughn Company
Austin, Texas

Published in the United States in 1990 by Steck-Vaughn Co.,
Austin, Texas, a subsidiary of National Education Corporation.

A Cherrytree Book

Designed and produced by
A S Publishing

Picture Credits Bridgeman Art
Library frontispiece,
pps 7, 11, 17, 19, 45 (bottom),
47; Mansell
Collection p9; Marshall Arts
pps 20, 23;
National Portrait Gallery pps
25, 27; New York
Historical Society p31.

Library of Congress Cataloging-in-Publication Data

Clarke, Brenda, 1946–
    Fighting for their faith / by Brenda Clarke : illustrated by
Andrew Howat.
        p.   cm. — (Tales of courage)
    Summary: Describes the lives of various individuals throughout
history who lived and fought for their faith, including Saint
Francis of Assisi, Sir Thomas More, and Martin Luther King, Jr.
    ISBN 0-8114-2753-6
    1. Religious biography—Juvenile literature.   2. Martyrs—
Biography—Juvenile literature.   3. Saints—Biography—Juvenile
literature.   4. Missionaries—Biography—Juvenile literature.
[1. Reformers.   2. Saints.   3. Missionaries.   4. Martyrs.]
I. Howatt, Andrew, ill.   II. Title.   III. Series.
BL72.C52   1990
291'.092'2—dc20
[920]   89-71372
                                                   CIP
                                                    AC

Printed in Italy by New Interlitho
Bound in the United States
1   2   3   4   5   6   7   8   9   0   IL   94   93   92   91   90

□ CONTENTS □

□ COURAGE TO FIGHT □

When Thomas More defied the wrath of King Henry VIII by refusing to acknowledge him as head of the Church of England, he knew very well that the king's anger might cost him his life. Similarly, Martin Luther, when he publicly spoke out against what he saw as errors in the Church, knew that he might put himself in danger.

In every religion, in countries all over the world, there have been people brave enough to stand up alone and avow their faith when others mocked or threatened them. People who have died for their beliefs are known as martyrs, and in the annals of Christianity there have been many. The early Christians faced cruel persecution. Stephen was stoned to death; Peter was crucified. In Rome Christians were forced to worship in underground catacombs, and many died horribly, mauled by wild animals for sport, rather than abandon their faith.

The religious teachers and prophets — Jesus, Muhammad, Buddha, and those who followed them — demonstrated courage in their lives, work, and teachings. They fought to change people's lives, and to win their hearts and minds. Their teachings, and those of other great world religions, such as Judaism, Hinduism, and Sikhism, continue to inspire men and women today, especially in those countries where the practice of any form of religion is outlawed.

It takes courage to stand out from the crowd, to disagree with the opinions of others. George Fox, the seventeenth-century founder of the Quakers, was often mocked and ill-treated as he preached. So, a century later, was the Methodist John Wesley who rode on horseback through England, preaching in the fields and on street corners. Wesley took his faith across the Atlantic, to America, as the Pilgrims had done. They went in search of freedom of conscience, a freedom for which many people have fought and still fight today.

The missionaries

Missionaries have risked extraordinary physical dangers to spread the teachings of religion and to do other good works, such as healing the sick, freeing the enslaved, and caring for those whom others despise and reject.

In the sixth century a Benedictine abbot named Augustine was summoned to see Pope Gregory the Great. The Pope had seen children with fair hair and blue eyes in the slave markets of Rome. He was told that the children came from the heathen island of Britain, a wild and barbarous land, little changed by its period of Roman rule. It had now fallen back into paganism under its new invaders, the Angles and Saxons.

Gregory could not believe such children could be savages. Their faces remained in his memory, and later he decided to send Augustine to England, to restore Christianity among the Angles and Saxons. Augustine was afraid, and when he reached France, he heard such frightening tales about the barbarism of the English that he wanted to turn around and hurry back to Rome.

Pope Gregory discovers pagan English slaves in Rome.

Pope Gregory told Augustine to conquer his fear, and the missionary crossed the English Channel to land in Kent in A.D. 597. After he had converted King Ethelbert, people came from far and near to hear him preach. He had conquered fear, and so begun his great work.

Fighting for freedom and faith

Religious believers have been persecuted for their faith in many lands. We read in the Old Testament of the Jews' captivity in Babylon and Egypt, and of how Moses led them to the Promised Land.

Two hundred years before the birth of Jesus Christ, the Jews faced persecution again. Their Seleucid (Greek) rulers tried to turn Palestine into a wholly Greek state. They forbade the Jews to observe the Sabbath day and made them eat pork, a food Jews regard as unclean.

The Jews rose in revolt, led by a priest named Mattathias and his sons, one of whom was Judas Maccabaeus ("The Hammer"). Today, Jews celebrate Hannukah, the Festival of Lights, in memory of the revolt. By 129 B.C. they had won their independence, but it was short-lived. In 63 B.C. the Romans made Palestine part of their empire.

A Jewish group known as the Zealots

led the patriotic resistance movement against the Romans. One of Jesus's disciples, Simon, was a Zealot, but Jesus told his followers to turn away from violence – just as he told Peter to put down his sword when the soldiers came to arrest Jesus.

In A.D. 66 the Jewish rebellion reached a climax. The Roman Army marched to quell the revolt; Jerusalem was taken and its temple destroyed in A.D. 70. All that remains of this ancient holy site today is the Wailing Wall, a place venerated by modern Jews.

The hilltop fortress of Masada was the last stronghold of the Jewish resistance. Besieged by the Roman Tenth Legion, the defenders held out for months. When the Romans broke through the defenses, they found only bodies. More than 900 defenders were dead, killed by ten chosen men rather than be captured. Only two women and five children were alive.

Religious wars

Wars started by religious quarrels have caused great suffering. The two great faiths of Christianity and Islam both regard Jerusalem as a holy city, as do the Jews. Because of this, Christians and Muslims fought a long series of medieval wars, known as the Crusades, for control of the Holy Land.

There were deeds of great bravery and chivalry on both sides – and also much that was shameful and wrong. This was the era of the Crusader kings, St. Louis of France and Richard the Lionheart of England, and of the great Muslim leader Saladin. Religious orders of warrior knights, known as the Knights Templars and Hospitalers, were formed to fight in these troubled times.

Courageous in resistance

Sometimes it takes great courage and religious faith not to fight. In the 1980s the Indian Sikh leader Sant Harchand Longowal spoke out against the violent extremists who wished to fight the Indian Army. He was murdered to silence his opposition. Martin Luther King, Jr., the American civil rights leader, was inspired by the nonviolent ideals of the Indian nationalist Mahatma Gandhi. Gandhi urged his followers not to hate their enemies; but to hate only the evils in society bred by injustice and wrongdoing. Gandhi was born a Hindu. Martin Luther King was a Baptist. Both were assassinated for their beliefs.

The fight for civil rights in South Africa has been led by churchmen such as Alan Boesak and Desmond Tutu. Boesak is a minister in the Dutch Reformed Church, and he has said that, "to be a Christian in South Africa today you have to be engaged in the struggle – there is no middle ground."

Cardinal Jozsef Mindszenty challenged the Hungarian Communist government in the 1940s. When the Communists, who tried to ban the practice of all religion, seized power in Eastern Europe after World War II, many believers faced hardships, imprisonment, and even death for their faith. The Cardinal refused to allow the Communists to take charge of church schools; for this he was found guilty of treason and jailed from 1949 to 1956. Briefly freed, he then took refuge in the United States Embassy, refusing to leave Hungary until 1971, four years before his death.

Martin Niemoller, too, spent years in jail, as a prisoner of the Nazis in Germany. He had served in the German

Navy during the World War I, but spoke out boldly against the Nazis in the 1930s. Many German churchpeople were too afraid to stand up to Hitler, but Pastor Niemoller showed no fear and organized a church movement against the Nazis. Jailed in 1938, he was imprisoned in the Sachsenhausen and Dachau concentration camps until freed in 1945.

Maximilian Kolbe was proclaimed a saint in 1982. Born in 1894, this Polish priest fought off the effects of tuberculosis to found a monastery. He planned to use modern technology – films and pilot-priests – to spread the Gospel. But in 1939 came war. He might have escaped imprisonment by claiming he was as German as his name. But Father Kolbe was adamant that he was Polish. He was arrested by the Gestapo and sent to Auschwitz concentration camp.

In 1941 Kolbe died. He had been beaten and ill-treated like other inmates of Auschwitz. At last, he gave his life to save another prisoner, volunteering to take the man's place in a terrible concrete "living tomb." Father Kolbe, with barely one good lung, prayed and sang with his fellow sufferers. He was finally killed with a poisonous injection and his body burned in the camp crematorium.

Fighters for their beliefs

In the modern world, religious persecution can be just as harsh as in previous centuries, when dissenters risked torture on the rack and death at the stake. Christians and Muslims have suffered terribly in Communist Albania, which proclaimed itself the world's first "atheist state" in 1967. In the 1930s about 70 percent of Albanians were Muslims, and the rest were Christians. Since the Com-

Christians and Muslims fought fiercely for control of the Holy Land.

munist takeover, many mosques and churches have been destroyed, and priests imprisoned and executed. Despite this, men and women of both faiths continue to practice their religion in secret.

When we read stories about such brave people as Oscar Romero of El Salvador and Janani Luwum of Uganda, we recall the famous martyrs and faith-fighters of the past. The belief in what is right, in what is true and good, still strengthens and inspires those with the faith – and the courage – to stand up in the face of evil.

□ THE GREAT MISSIONARY □

Saul of Tarsus was a Jew zealous to stamp out the new Christian religion. He watched with approval as a mob stoned to death Stephen, the first Christian martyr. Then, converted by a miraculous vision, and renamed Paul, he risked sharing Stephen's fate to spread his new faith.

Saul of Tarsus was praying when he heard footsteps on the stairs. The door opened. He turned toward the sound, even though now that he was blind he could not see his visitor. Then he felt a hand laid on his head and the visitor spoke. In that instant, Saul miraculously regained his sight.

The visitor, a man called Ananias, looked at him wonderingly. Was this the Saul of Tarsus whose arrival all the Christians in Damascus had been dreading? The man who had persecuted Christians in Jerusalem and had come to Damascus with orders to do the same?

Saul becomes Paul

Then Saul began to speak. His first request was to be baptized as a Christian in the name of Paul. He told the astonished Ananias about his wondrous experience on the road to Damascus: how a light had blinded him and how he had heard the voice of Christ.

Soon, Paul was preaching in the synagogues, to the amazement of both Christians and Jews. Here he was, boldly proclaiming his Christianity when only weeks before he had been actively trying to stamp out the new faith.

The strict Jews argued with Paul, but he would not be silenced. So they plotted to get rid of him. A Christian friend heard rumors of a plot to kill Paul, and plans were made for his escape.

The city gates were guarded night and day by Paul's enemies, but the Christians had become used to avoiding watchful eyes. They found a house built close to the city wall, and one dark night they took Paul there and hid him in a large basket. They attached it to a strong rope and lowered him out of a window, down to the ground outside the city wall. It was Paul's first narrow escape from death.

Paul's great journeys

After preaching for some time, Paul went to Jerusalem and met the apostles Peter and James. They realized that Paul was a man of action, and that he would be the person to undertake the great and dangerous task of taking Christianity to the non-Jewish world – the Gentiles.

Paul was not afraid to argue even with Peter, the leader of Jesus's followers. He believed Christianity was a religion for all people, not just Jews. So he set out on his travels, journeying on foot and over the Mediterranean Sea to preach the new faith. There were many perils. Paul was sometimes ill. He was driven out of cities many times. He was stoned and left for dead. Often he had to run from angry mobs. He was flogged and flung into prison. He must have had a great deal of stamina, to travel so far, speaking, writing letters, and always encouraging his fellow Christians to remain steadfast.

St. Paul was rescued off the coast of Malta after his ship was wrecked in a storm. He stayed on the island for three months, preaching to the inhabitants.

While preaching in Jerusalem itself, he was attacked by an angry crowd, and barely rescued by Roman soldiers who arrested him. Since he was a Roman citizen, Paul claimed the right to trial in Rome. While being taken under guard to Rome, his vessel was shipwrecked on the island of Malta. The sailors despaired, as the storm waves broke over the little vessel, but Paul told them all would be well. They spent three months on Malta before they could continue their journey to Rome.

We do not know what happened when Paul finally reached Rome, or how Paul died. Tradition says that he met a martyr's death during the reign of the emperor Nero (A.D. 54-68). What we do know is that the growth of the Christian church into a worldwide organization was mainly due to the courageous spirit and zealous efforts of a dedicated convert, St. Paul.

□ BRAVING THE PAGANS □

After the Roman Empire was overrun in the fifth century by barbarians, Christianity in Europe seemed to be imperiled.

Boniface grasped the axe handle and looked up at the huge oak tree. He must bring it down swiftly with a few mighty strokes, or else these surly Germans might decide to fell him instead.

They were standing in one of the sacred groves which the Germans regarded with such awe. Boniface knew the power of the old pagan myths. The Germans kept this grove for worship of the great thunder-god Thor, and this magnificent tree was his oak.

The monk from England had told them that Thor's power was at an end. He brought news of the one great God of the Christians, and in his name he would show them that Thor was a false god, with no strength. He would cut down the oak and Thor would do nothing to prevent it. Nor would he harm Boniface.

Boniface swung the axe again and again. The oak creaked, tottered, and crashed to earth. The fierce, pagan warriors looked on in wonder. There was no thunderclap from Thor's hammer, no lightning flash. This monk, long-robed like a woman, was unscathed. He had broken the power of the old Nordic gods.

Destroying old idols
Boniface destroyed many other pagan idols during his mission to the German tribes. Yet he was a scholarly man, expected to rise to a high position in the church at home in England. Instead, he had asked the Pope to send him among the warlike pagans of Europe to win them for Christ.

Knowing that he needed powerful allies, he gained the support of Charles Martel, leader of the neighboring Christian Franks. The German tribes, who had fought against the mighty legions of Rome, knew and feared the strength of Martel. Boniface guessed they would respect also a monk who could call on the friendship and military might of such a heroic warrior.

The death of Boniface
Although Boniface worked hard to establish Christianity among the Germans, he was not entirely successful. Many of the early missionaries in Europe found that converts slipped back into the old religion. When he was almost 80, Boniface returned to the Frisians, the people among whom he had begun his work so many years before.

One day in A.D. 754, he prepared to baptize a group of new Christians beside a river. Suddenly, with wild shouts and pagan oaths, a band of axe-wielding tribesmen rushed upon Boniface and his companions and killed them.

It was a death feared by many missionaries. Boniface had carried his Christian message fearlessly to the fiercest tribes of Europe, and his pioneering work eventually bore fruit.

St. Boniface fells the sacred oak venerated by the pagan German tribes.

MUHAMMAD THE PROPHET

In the city of Mecca, Arabia, the prophet Muhammad proclaimed the new religion of Islam — "submission" to one God. He attracted a few loyal followers but also many enemies.

Ever since Muhammad had begun preaching that Allah was the one true God, the rich merchants who ruled Mecca had regarded him with suspicion. If his teaching gained hold, it might end the coming of pilgrims to Mecca to worship the many pagan idols at the sacred Kaaba. The pilgrims brought great wealth to the Meccans. If Muhammad grew too strong, he might eventually take their power and wealth from them.

Flight from Mecca
In the year 622, Muhammad fled from his home town, where his life was threatened. His friend and follower Abu Bakr journeyed with him and their guide southward to the mountains, knowing their enemies would expect them to ride north, to Yathrib, where Muhammad's followers already awaited him. The refugees found a cave to shelter in for some days, anxiously watching for the dust-clouds that would mean pursuit. Their guide knew the desert well and, when they felt it safe to move, he led them north by secret paths until, after 12 days of hard riding, they reached the welcoming oasis of Yathrib. For giving shelter to Muhammad, Yathrib was renamed Medina, the City of the Prophet; the year of his flight from Mecca, known as *hejira*, is the date from which Muslims begin their calendar.

The Muslims fight for survival
The Muslims at Medina were poor. Many had left all their possessions in Mecca to join Muhammad in exile. It was a dangerous time, with many violent blood feuds between warring families. Raiding was a way of life. To help feed

his hungry followers, Muhammad himself led raids on Meccan merchant caravans traveling across the desert.

Muhammad had to fight for his survival and that of the new faith of Islam. In one battle, 3,000 Meccans attacked 1,000 Muslims, Muhammad was wounded, and many of his followers killed. But no enemies would silence his prophecy.

In 627 an army of 10,000 Meccans laid siege to Medina but Muhammad and his followers held out. He ordered every basket of food to be brought in to the storehouses, and had a ditch dug to defend the oasis against enemy cavalry. The siege lasted two weeks. Fodder for the horses and camels ran out. Then, after a terrible night of storm, the great Meccan army melted away.

Winning all for Islam

Muhammad now set out to win even his enemies to Islam. Meccan power began to weaken, as more and more people joined the Prophet. In 628 he decided to go to Mecca in person, as a peaceful pilgrim. The Meccans agreed that the following year he could enter the city. In 630 he came again with all his followers, and paraded in triumph around the sacred Kaaba, the ancient shrine. The old, pagan idols inside it were destroyed. The "Time of Ignorance" was at an end and the Kaaba, once venerated by pagans, became the focus of pilgrimage for Muslims worshipping Allah, the one God. His task done, Muhammad died in 632.

Hundreds of Muhammad's followers joined him in exile in Medina. They fought for their survival in this desert oasis by raiding merchant caravans.

□ TURNING THE TIDE □

Within 100 years of Muhammad's death, Islam had spread through the Middle East to North Africa, Asia, and Europe, where Spain had fallen to Muslim invaders by 714. Islamic warriors seemed set to push farther into European lands.

The autumn mist of a cold October morning hung about the trees and rolled across the low ground. Each man in the line waited expectantly for orders — shield firm in hand, weapon at the ready. Once more the Frankish army faced battle; this time against not only a rival army but a rival faith.

The Franks lived in what we now call France and Germany. They were a powerful people, giving allegiance to their overlord, Charles, son of Pepin. He had proved a worthy leader, who had secured his borders by victories over neighboring tribes — Frisians, Saxons, Bavarians, and rival Franks — so that his own people might live without fear of invasion.

Charles had the support of the Christian church, in return for helping the missionaries Willibrord and Boniface with their work among the pagan Germans who lived to the east. Peace and civilization were spreading in northern Europe, but now the new Christian faith faced a further threat from outside — the Muslim Moors of Spain.

The Franks awaited them now, these fierce warriors from North Africa who with victory after victory had taken the Spanish lands of the Visigoths. Since then, rumors had come of Moors crossing the Pyrenees Mountains to raid near their southern borders, mounting swift attacks to see what resistance the Franks might offer. In 725 their invasions had reached as far north as Burgundy. If nobody stopped them, they would overrun the whole of western Europe and make these lands subject to Islam.

The Moors advance

In 732 the test came. Abd-al-Rahman, governor of Cordoba, led his Moorish army against Duke Eudes of Aquitaine. Desperately the Duke's men tried to hold off the advance, but in vain. An exhausted messenger had carried the news to the Franks with an urgent appeal to Charles to take the field.

Summoning his lords and his fighting men, Charles acted swiftly. Horses and warriors moved through thick woods and across fast-flowing rivers. Infantrymen carried spear, shield, bow and arrows, and the short, heavy, single-edged sword that they wielded with such skill. On these men rested the future of Christendom in western Europe. A party of Moors had advanced north to Poitiers, another seemed to be aiming for Tours. Now the opposing armies had met.

Behind the shieldwall, the Franks awaited first sight of an unknown and fearsome enemy. Their priests prayed for strength and courage at this time of trial. The Bishop had blessed them, and beside their lord's standard stood the cross. If the shieldwall stayed firm, Charles — and God — would bring them victory.

When the Moorish attack came, it was

fierce and bloody. But the Franks stood their ground. Again and again came waves of Islamic warriors calling with blood-curdling cries on the name of Allah. The Franks looked to their lord's banner and the cross, and pressed forward. The Moors wavered, then fell back, and the Franks pursued them, swords slashing. Back and back retreated the Moors, toward Poitiers.

Charles mustered his army for a final attack before nightfall. But Abd-al-Rahman was dead, and the fury of the Moorish onslaught with him. As the sky dark-ened, the exhausted warriors left the field for their camps.

In the morning, the Franks returned for battle, but the Moors had gone. For his victories, Charles earned the name Martel ("the Hammer") and his brave deeds were wound into legends told throughout Europe.

The Islamic warriors, the Moors, gather their forces for battle outside the French city of Tours. After conquering Spain, they hoped to gain control of Frankish lands.

□ SOLDIERS OF THE FAITHS □

The warriors of Christendom and Islam fought on. Soldiers from Europe – the Crusaders – wrested Jerusalem from Muslim control in 1099. Then the great Muslim leader Saladin led his armies into *jihad* (holy war) to regain the Holy Land.

The day was already heavy with heat. Young Al-Afdal, awake since before daybreak, watched and listened as the camp prepared for battle. His father, the Muslim leader Saladin, was supervising his troops. Arrows had been given to the archers, and snipers sent to pick off any Christian soldiers wandering about in search of water. The Muslim army's own water supplies had been brought from the Sea of Galilee, but Saladin had the Christians surrounded and cut off from the lake. To aggravate their enemies' parched throats, the Muslims had lit fires in the scrub.

For some time, a truce had existed between Christians and Muslims in the Holy Land, and caravans laden with silks and spices once more crossed the desert. But such wealth tempted the greed of the Frankish lord Reynald of Chatillon. In 1186 he attacked a huge caravan from Cairo, making off with an enormous haul of booty. The truce was broken and Saladin prepared for his *jihad*.

In May 1187, the Muslim leader gathered the largest host he had ever commanded. Guy of Lusignan, Christian king of Jerusalem, responded by summoning all the men he could muster. The Hospitalers and Templars (orders of religious knights sworn to defend the Holy Land) sent him most of their soldiers. From Jerusalem, the much-revered relic of the True Cross was sent to accompany the Christian army.

Saladin prepares

Saladin was ready. He marched his troops across the Jordan River to attack the town of Tiberias, which was defended by the wife of a Christian noble. The chivalrous knights of the Hospitalers and Templars wanted at once to go to her aid. Others thought it wiser to remain camped where they were, at Sephoria, because there was plenty of water and pasture for the horses. Saladin would never risk attacking them there. But the Templars persuaded King Guy that this was a strategy for cowards, and so the Christians set off for Tiberias.

Saladin's scouts brought him news of their move while he was at prayer. He led his army to a village called Hattin, blocking the Christians' road.

On a hot, stifling morning the Christians left the cool of Sephoria to march across the bare hills to Tiberias. There was no shade and no water. They sweated in their armor. Horses and men were parched with thirst. Their pace slowed. Muslim snipers harassed them with showers of arrows. By late afternoon the Crusaders were exhausted. They had reached the plain above Hattin; ahead lay a rocky hill, and below was the village and the lake. The Templars begged for rest and the army camped, but the only well they found was dry.

Saladin, the great Muslim leader during the medieval wars of the Crusades.

Battle in the heat

Saladin waited throughout the night, and lit his fires. He had already cut off the enemy's retreat.

At daybreak, Christians desperate for water surged toward the lake, but flames from Saladin's brush fires drove them back. Dazzled by sun, blinded by smoke, and choked by heat, many were slaughtered. Saladin and his young son watched the thirst-driven Christian knights as they fought with desperate courage to drive back Muslim cavalry charges. The attack pressed on and on up the hill of Hattin until at last King Guy's knights gathered around his red tent on the hilltop for their last stand.

The memory of their heroism remained with Al-Afdal: "When the Frankish king had withdrawn to the hilltop, his knights made a gallant charge and drove the Muslims back upon my father. I watched his dismay." Saladin rushed forward to encourage his men, who once more drove their enemy up the hill. But again the knights rallied and charged. "We have not beaten them so long as that tent stands there," said the Muslim leader. And as he spoke the red tent of the Christian king was overturned. Saladin dismounted, bowed low, and thanked Allah for his victory.

The True Cross had fallen to the infidel and was lost to Christendom forever. Saladin himself struck off the head of the truce-breaker Reynald of Chatillon, and ordered the slaying of the captive Templar and Hospitaler knights. King Guy and the remaining Crusaders he spared. Now lord of the Muslim world, Saladin marched his army through Palestine and Syria and on October 2, 1187, he captured Jerusalem. He had restored the Holy Land to Islam.

19

□ JOAN OF ARC □

Joan of Arc kneels before the Dauphin Charles of France.

Called by God, Joan of Arc led armies into battle, yet she had no hatred in her heart for the enemies of France. In the end, she died rather than deny what she believed were divine commandments.

The courtroom was hushed, waiting for the young girl to answer the Inquisitor's next question. She looked so pale and thin, after weeks of imprisonment, without sunlight, exercise, or proper food. But she faced her persecutors fearlessly, her eyes bright.

The Inquisitor tried once again.

"Joan, you have agreed to put on women's clothes again, and to obey the rules of the church."

The girl nodded.

"Will you now also state before us all that you were mistaken, that you did not hear voices from God?"

She shook her head. "I cannot say something did not happen when it did." The Inquisitor turned away. There was no more to be said. The girl had condemned herself. But only one man in the court showed any sign of triumph: Pierre Cauchon, Bishop of Beauvais, who had never believed that this girl had been called by God. He smiled, gloating at his apparent victory. He was about to silence the Maid of Orléans forever.

The girl from Domrémy

Joan's amazing story began in 1425, when she was 13. A simple peasant girl in a country village, she had never known lasting peace, for France was being torn apart by the Hundred Years' War. The armies of England and Burgundy occupied much of French territory. The once-rich countryside was ravaged by famine and pestilence. France did not even have a king worthy of the name.

One summer's day Joan heard voices from God. They first spoke to her while she was tending sheep in her home village of Domrémy. Suddenly, she was dazzled by a brilliant radiance, and she heard a loving voice telling her to be virtuous and say her prayers. Shortly afterward, she saw a vision. St. Michael, St. Catherine, and St. Margaret appeared to her and told her that she was destined to leave her village and restore the rightful king to the French throne.

Her first task was to gain an audience with the Dauphin Charles, the prince whom she must make King of France. First she persuaded the local military governor to help her. He feared Joan might be a witch, and insisted that a priest question her. The priest was soon convinced that Joan was no witch, and she was given an armed escort.

In February 1429 she bade farewell to her family and rode off to see the Dauphin at his castle in Chinon. She was disguised as a boy, her hair cropped short, for the journey took them through dangerous territory. At Chinon, the prince

was in hiding, afraid and disheartened. His courtiers scoffed at the news that a peasant girl was coming to see him. What next? But when Joan picked out Charles (whom she had never seen) from the crowd of courtiers, they fell silent. Joan knelt at his feet, saying she had come to help him secure his rightful crown, and Charles took heart.

A maid rallies France

Joan's arrival at court had a miraculous effect on French morale. She won over even the most cynical army commanders by her shining faith. Armored like a soldier, she rode forth at the head of Charles's small but revitalized army. She would, she told him, lead the French to victory at Orléans.

The city of Orléans was besieged by an English army. Joan led several hundred troops, with supplies of food and gunpowder, across the Loire River in boats and entered the city right under the noses of the encircling English.

Her arrival roused the defenders to new efforts. Joan was everywhere, encouraging everyone. Tough, hard-swearing soldiers fell to their knees as she rode by on her charger. Single-handedly she rallied the French forces, convincing the soldiers that victory was certain.

The French attacked the English forts around the city. Joan was in the vanguard of the French rush. In the thick of the battle, the French men-at-arms followed her shining figure, armor bright, banner streaming in the wind. Even when she was wounded in the shoulder by an arrow, she urged her companions on to win the day. The attack faltered without her, and so when her wound had been roughly bandaged, Joan ran back into the forefront of the battle.

The English were overrun, and their army scattered. Orléans was freed, and the exultant French marched back into their city cheering their new heroine, the Maid of Orléans.

After this great French victory in 1429, the English and their Burgundian allies fell back and Frenchmen flocked to join Joan's army. Charles was triumphantly crowned king in Rheims Cathedral, and Joan stood close by him during the ceremony. Without her, Charles would never have won his crown. Yet she refused all honors and riches.

Joan is betrayed

The English spread lies about Joan, saying she must be a witch. How else could she have turned the war against them? They were desperate to get rid of her. So, too, were some of the French nobles and churchmen who had joined forces with the English.

Joan hated to see the terrible devastation that war had brought to her beloved France. She redoubled her efforts to bring peace. In May 1430 she was captured at the town of Compiègne. Leading a raid outside the town she became separated from her comrades and was dragged from her horse. She was never to be free again.

Her Burgundian captors sold her to the English for gold. King Charles had no courage without Joan, and was too weak even to try to pay a ransom for her release. She had committed no crime, but she was accused of being a witch and of disobeying the church. So she was handed over to Bishop Cauchon, her unrelenting enemy, to be tried in a church court. After she tried to escape by leaping from a window, Joan was kept in chains and watched constantly by soldiers.

A symbol of patriotism

The written report of Joan's trial shows how calmly and bravely she answered all the false charges brought against her. She vowed she had no quarrel with the church. Yes, she would give up wearing boy's clothes as was demanded. But what her voices told her must remain secret. She could not deny her voices, for she believed they came from God. Even when threatened with the terrible death-sentence imposed on heretics (enemies of the church), she would not give ground.

On May 30, 1431, Joan was burned at the stake in Rouen's market place. She met her death courageously, holding in her hands a small wooden cross given to her by an English soldier in the crowd. Even the English king's secretary was moved by her death, writing that, "We have burned a good and holy person." Joan's enemies were still so fearful that they ordered her ashes scattered in the river so that no trace of her remained.

But nothing could obliterate Joan's life and deeds. Her blazing courage had lit a fire in French hearts, and although she did not live to see it, final victory for France was assured. She became France's greatest symbol of patriotism. In 1456 the church declared her innocent of all the charges brought against her. In 1920 she was canonized, becoming Saint Joan. Memorials to Joan can be seen in churches all over France.

Clad in armor and carrying the French banner, Joan leads the attack against the English at Orléans.

THE CHURCH DIVIDED

Who was right – the Pope or the Protestant leaders Martin Luther and John Calvin? During the years of religious argument known as the Reformation, many brave people chose to die rather than deny their beliefs.

By the sixteenth century many people felt that the Christian church had lost its way. Too many priests seemed worldly and corrupt, willing to pardon people for their sins in return for payment. A movement began to reform the church, led by those who protested against such abuses – and therefore called Protestantism. In 1517 Martin Luther, a German friar, challenged abuses in the church. He had expected the church leaders to agree with him, but instead found himself accused of heresy. Luther believed all people could find Christian faith in the Bible directly, without need of popes and bishops to explain it. In Switzerland, John Calvin and Huldrych Zwingli preached similar ideas.

In England, the Reformation was hastened by King Henry VIII's desire for a divorce, denied him by the Pope.

□ THE TRIAL OF THOMAS MORE □

The air felt fresh after the dark staleness of the prison cell. A murmur came from the crowd as the condemned man appeared, but after that there was silence. As they approached the scaffold, the guards stood back, and in the shadow of the Tower of London, Sir Thomas More walked toward the waiting executioner.

The London crowd knew why More must die. Unable to sacrifice his faith and conscience as the king demanded, instead he was sacrificing himself. The king's wife of many years had borne just one child, Princess Mary. Henry wanted a son to succeed him. He also had a new love, Anne Boleyn, whom he wanted to marry. He had applied to the Pope for a divorce, but the Pope refused. Enraged, Henry declared that henceforth the Pope had no authority in England and that he, as king, was now also head of the English Church. Protestants supported Henry's break with Rome, but many other subjects felt that their allegiance belonged to the Pope.

Sir Thomas More was the king's most brilliant minister. He was also a man of virtue, wisdom, understanding, and kindness. Impressed by his skill as a lawyer, Henry made Thomas More his Lord Chancellor, one of the most powerful men in the land. Henry needed More's support to gain acceptance for his changes to England's religion. Thomas could not give it.

More resigned as Lord Chancellor to live quietly at home. He would not publicly speak out against the king, but in 1534 Henry demanded that his subjects must swear an oath that he, not the Pope, was head of the church in England. Thomas More knew he could not do so. For this refusal, he was sent to the Tower of London.

Prison and the block
Thomas was kept in prison for a year be-

Sir Thomas More with his family. Around his neck hangs the Chancellor's gold chain of office. Sir Thomas was later beheaded for his principles.

fore his trial, but he remained calm and cheerful. His friends and family tried to make him change his mind about the oath, but he would not, though he knew it was likely to cost him his life.

When at last he was brought to trial, on charges of treason, false evidence was given against him. No one doubted the verdict of the jury would be "guilty." The judges (who included Anne Boleyn's father, brother, and uncle) sentenced More to a traitor's death – to be hanged, drawn, and quartered. The king spared him that, ordering that his former Chancellor be beheaded.

For five days Thomas More waited in his cell, praying and writing letters of farewell. Calm to the last, he joked with the Lieutenant of the Tower who helped him mount the scaffold. "See me safe up, and for my coming down let me shift for myself!" He spoke cheerfully to the executioner, and forgave the man for what he was about to do. After saying a prayer, he told the onlookers that he died "in the faith and for the faith of the Catholic Church, the king's good servant and God's first." Then he fixed the blindfold on his own eyes and knelt to die.

THOMAS CRANMER STANDS FAST

It was the spring of 1556. Thomas Cranmer, once archbishop of Canterbury, was a prisoner. It seemed that his life's work had been wasted. The new queen Mary, daughter of Henry VIII, was a devout Roman Catholic and determined to make England a Catholic country again. Cranmer had spent his career leading his country toward the Protestant faith, and the queen was demanding that he should declare in public that he had been wrong.

He had been arrested, along with two bishops named Ridley and Latimer, thrown into the Tower of London, and then forced to watch as Ridley and Latimer were burned to death at the stake, as heretics. Cranmer himself had been stripped of his office as archbishop and endured a long trial.

Cranmer had risen to success by supporting Henry VIII in seeking his divorce. The king liked and trusted him because he sought no rewards. He liked to remain outside the political wranglings of the court and work on church reforms and the new Protestant prayer book. Yet Cranmer alone dared to plead for those who fell into Henry's disfavor, including Thomas More and Anne Boleyn.

When Henry died, his young son became King Edward VI. Led by Cranmer, the Church of England grew strong. Cranmer produced a prayer book, written in English not Latin, and saw to it that every church was given a Bible, which was supremely important to Protestants. All seemed well, until the sickly Edward died in 1553 at the age of 17.

Now Cranmer was forced into politics, to try and stop Edward's half-sister Mary from becoming queen. But she did, and took her revenge.

Cranmer becomes a martyr
They humiliated the old man by making him sign papers that denied his beliefs. But his accusers were not satisfied with that. They showed him no mercy. He was sentenced to death and on March 21, 1556, they came to take him to the stake. But first they demanded that he make his denial in public. At this moment of defeat and death, Cranmer faced his enemies squarely and refused to do what they wanted.

He went to the stake with courage. As the fire flickered around him, Cranmer held the right hand that had signed the papers denying his Protestant faith steadily in the flames, saying "This hand hath offended. It shall first be burned."

RELIGIOUS WARS

Many other Protestant and Catholic martyrs were to follow More and Cranmer in dying for their beliefs. Some, like Edmund Campion and Margaret Clitherow, endured solitary trial and death. Thousands more died in the religious wars that divided Europe for over a century. In Germany the Emperor Charles V (1519-56) tried to crush Protestantism by force. Later came the terri-

Thomas Cranmer, Archbishop of Canterbury, who was burned at the stake for refusing to deny his Protestant faith.

ble Thirty Years War (1619-48), in which neither side gained victory. In France Catholics and Protestants fought each other from 1562 to 1598, when King Henry IV, a Calvinist turned Catholic, guaranteed toleration for the French Protestants or Huguenots.

Today, Catholics and Protestants still understand Christianity differently. They are closer than before, but their religious differences are still substantial. Nevertheless, dialogue between the two main branches of Christianity continues.

□ TRAVELERS FOR GOD □

Inspired by missionary fervor, Jesuit priests took the Christian faith to the Far East. As far as they could travel, men like Francis Xavier spread the word of God.

Ignatius Loyola (1491-1556) was a Spanish soldier. While recovering from a serious leg wound, he began reading about the life and teachings of Jesus Christ. It changed his life; he put away his sword and put on the clothes of a beggar to travel as a pilgrim to Jerusalem.

The Catholic Church had met the challenge of the Reformation by reorganizing itself. It welcomed the energy and courage of Loyola, his friend Francis Xavier, and five other followers who took vows of poverty, chastity, and obedience, and dedicated themselves to missionary work. In 1540 Pope Paul III permitted them to found a new order: the Society of Jesus, or Jesuits. Their work signaled the Counter Reformation and the revival of the Catholic Church.

To India and beyond

In 1497 the Portuguese Vasco da Gama had been the first European to sail to India around Africa. For European travelers, the voyage to the East was as long and hazardous as ever. For Christian missionaries, determined to convert the Indian people to the true faith, such a journey was doubly dangerous.

In 1541 Francis Xavier left Portugal for India. He was not the first choice for the mission. He had replaced a sick man. But he displayed total devotion to his cause. In seven years he placed 30 missionaries in India and Indonesia.

Life for a Christian missionary could never be easy. One was speared to death by a mob. Another was driven mad. Europeans found the Asian climate hard to bear. Fevers and other diseases struck down even the strongest men. In addition there were the hardships of traveling many miles on foot and by boat, as well as the hostility of local rulers.

Frustrated by what he saw as lack of success in India, Xavier's hopes were raised by traders' tales of China and Japan. No European had seen Japan until 1542, when a Portuguese ship was blown off course. Xavier determined to go east.

With a Japanese guide named Yajiro (an alleged murderer who became a Christian), Francis Xavier and two other Jesuits set out from Malacca (in modern Malaysia) by junk for the nine-week sea voyage to Japan.

Converting Japan

The Japanese were at first amused, then outraged at this European who came among them with his talk of crosses and resurrection. Xavier, however, was made of stern stuff — and showed it by running through the winter snow, singing as he did so. He walked barefoot in winter for almost 300 miles to seek an audience with the Japanese emperor, whom he hoped to convert. But the emperor had no real power and was so poor he charged a fee to each visitor.

Xavier therefore confronted one of Japan's many fearsome warlords, Yoshi-

Francis Xavier's courage in running barefoot through snow impressed this Japanese nobleman.

taka. Impressed by the Jesuits' courage, and the gift of a chiming clock, Yoshitaka allowed them the use of an unused Buddhist temple. Xavier was never afraid to argue his case, even when his comrades feared they might all be beheaded at any moment. People came in droves to the temple, to gaze at and talk to the foreigners – who were said by some to be Buddhists from the far West.

Xavier was not content to remain in Japan, constantly debating, seldom converting. If he could reach China, where the emperor had real power, and convert him, that would mean something. He took to the seas again, and finally landed on an island only 30 miles from the coast of China. But the ship he had chartered for the last leg of his journey never arrived. Worn out by his travels, he was too weak to withstand the onset of winter and, without proper shelter, died of exposure. Had he reached China, his plan was simple: to go to the emperor and "to declare the word of God."

□ NEW WORLD PILGRIMS □

In 1620, the *Mayflower* sailed from England. The Puritan Pilgrims on board were ready to face whatever hardships they would meet in the New World of America. Even if some died, and many did, the rest would be free to worship as they wished.

"Do not wander far!" Isaac Allerton warned his three children. All the newcomers to America were thankful for the spring sunshine after such a long and bitter winter. "Remember, we have work to do." Isaac knew they must work fast, to clear the forest, till the soil, and plant crops — or next winter, more people would perish from hunger and disease. Many had already died, including Mary Allerton, the young mother of his three children — Bartholomew, Remember, and Mary.

Nervously, the children explored the forest, keeping in sight of the tiny settlement. They knew well the tales of wolves, bears, and other wild animals, and of savage Indians who skinned their captives alive and roasted human flesh.

The Allerton children prayed every night for strength to survive in this frightening wilderness. They prayed too for their friend, Priscilla Mullins, who was now an orphan. She had lost her father, mother, and brother. Governor John Carver's wife was dead, and so was Captain Miles Standish's wife Rose. There were many men without wives after that first winter. But the Puritans had known hardship before, and learned how to endure it.

Pilgrims to a New World

The *Mayflower* Pilgrims were not the first European settlers in America — Sir Walter Raleigh had founded a short-lived colony in North Carolina in 1585. Later settlers, in Jamestown, Virginia (1607), had faced dreadful hardships. Two-thirds of them died of hunger or sickness. The native Indians, seeing that these newcomers meant to take their land, fought fiercely to defend it.

The *Mayflower* had brought settlers who sought freedom. In England Puritans were banned from working as teachers, clergymen, or government officials. Their religious beliefs were different from those of the King and the Church of England. They wanted to follow the teachings of the Bible without the instruction of priests and bishops, and to worship and live simply in a life dedicated to prayer and hard work.

The children had been excited when they first boarded ship in Plymouth. The *Mayflower* was only 100 feet long, and its passengers were crammed on deck, without cabins or anywhere dry to sleep. One pilgrim had been swept overboard by a wave; he lived only by clinging onto a rope until rescued with a boat hook.

When they landed in America, after nine weeks at sea, they gave thanks for their deliverance. America was a vast wilderness. Its dark forests were said to hide Indians, whose savagery was feared, but no Indians showed themselves at first. Even so no one slept soundly those first nights ashore and the men kept their muskets loaded.

Hunger and hardship

In their first winter, starvation was the colonists' worst enemy. They grew thin on meager rations of corn bread, wildfowl, and shellfish. Without proper houses, some people lived in holes in the ground, roofed over with turf. Half of the company died because of such hardships.

So it was good to be alive this spring morning in 1621. But the Allerton children were still on their guard. Hearing shouts, they ran back to the settlement. Was it an attack by Indians? To their surprise, they saw a stranger; an Indian named Samoset who spoke some English. It was the Puritans' first friendly encounter with their neighbors.

The Puritans built houses and that autumn they enjoyed the fruits of their first harvest, thanks to the Indians who had taught them how to plant crops that would grow in this new land. The survivors – Isaac Allerton, his children, and the others – enjoyed a feast of Thanksgiving for the harvest. Their Indian friends joined the celebration.

The Pilgrims' courage and faith had seen them through. A start had been made. Theirs was a modest victory; but they never lost faith in their eventual triumph. The colony's governor William Bradford described it this way, "As one candle may light a thousand, so the light here kindled has shown to many . . ."

Pilgrims making their way to church on a wintry morning. The men carried muskets in case of attack by hostile Indian tribes.

☐ MISSIONARY HERO ☐

Throughout the centuries, missionaries have braved dangers and hardships to spread their faith. They have journeyed far and wide. Jean de Brébeuf went to the forests and lakes of North America to convert the Indians.

The elderly Jesuit smiled at the eagerness of the young man sitting before him. "So you really want to go to New France, Jean? Be warned. It is a wild land very far from your home in Normandy. But there is much work to be done there."

The year was 1625. Jean de Brébeuf had been a Jesuit priest for only two years, and he was about to embark on a perilous mission. He was to sail to North America, to Canada (New France) to teach Christianity to the Indians.

The voyage gave the young man pause for thought. The Atlantic was stormy, and the small vessel was wave-tossed for weeks. Once ashore, Jean found himself a stranger in a vast wilderness of forest, rivers, and lakes. There were no roads — only winding forest trails — and no towns. A handful of Europeans lived in scattered forts and trading posts. Jean was sent to preach among a tribe who had greeted the French explorer Jacques Cartier almost a century earlier. The French jokingly called these Indians Hurons, or "bristleheads," because of their brushlike haircuts.

The Hurons' life-long enemies were the warlike Iroquois, another tribe living around the Great Lakes. The Iroquois scorned any peaceful dealings with the French and constantly raided Huron territory. Jean learned that, living among the forest Indians, even a priest had to learn some woodcraft to survive.

Studying Indian ways

After five years, he returned to France, forced to abandon his missionary work because of quarrels between the French and British, who both sought to control Canada. But in 1634 he was back in the forests, traveling on foot and by canoe, Bible in hand. He studied Indian ways, and wrote a grammar book and a catechism in the Huron language.

In 1638 the Jesuits founded a mission southeast of Georgian Bay, an inlet of Lake Huron in Ontario. Jean and his priests thanked the Lord when the Iroquois at last made peace with France in 1647. But joy was short-lived, for the savage Indians continued to attack their old Huron enemies. In 1648 war bands destroyed the mission and murdered many Hurons. In March 1649 near the

fort of St. Ignace, Father Brébeuf and another Jesuit missionary, Gabriel Lalemant, were captured by the Iroquois.

The Indians might have spared them if they had denied their Christian faith. But despite horrible tortures, Father Brébeuf never flinched. Stoned and bleeding, he was "baptized" with boiling water and then burned to death. He showed no fear and uttered no cry of pain: the Iroquois were so impressed by his courage that afterward they ate his heart — in order to acquire the same courage themselves.

Today St. Jean de Brébeuf (he was made a saint in 1930) is remembered with pride as the patron saint of Canada.

The Jesuit Father Brébeuf faces martyrdom as a captive of the Iroquois Indians. His Christian faith gave him the courage to die without flinching.

□ THE SMALL WOMAN □

Gladys Aylward had a price on her head – 100 dollars to be paid by the Japanese army for information leading to the capture of "The Small Woman," known as Ai-We-Deh, The Virtuous One.

Since arriving from England ten years ago Gladys Aylward had worked as a missionary in northwest China. Now her adopted country was at war, and her town under attack. Not knowing what to do she opened her Bible, and read at random a line of Chinese characters "Flee ye, flee ye into the mountains."

She escaped just in time, racing out of the city's back gate as Japanese troops marched in through the front. But she was seen. Bullets whined and cracked all around her; then a sharp blow on her back laid her flat.

She wriggled free of her thick, padded coat and, resting on the Bible that had fallen with her, slid toward the safety of the city's dry moat. Then she edged slowly backward into a field of tall, green wheat. Once well hidden, she fell asleep.

The thick, padded coat had saved her life. Her shoulder was only grazed. When she awoke, she hurried toward the town of Yangcheng, to the Inn of Eight Happinesses. Gladys had opened the Inn, with an older missionary named Mrs. Lawson, when she had arrived in China in 1930. Mrs. Lawson thought good food and story-telling, which the Chinese loved, would attract the men who led mule trains across the mountains. The men came for food and lodging – and heard stories from the Bible.

It took Gladys two days to reach Yangcheng, scrambling up rocks and down valleys. But now her purpose was clear.

Gladys Aylward distributes her meager rations among the war-orphaned Chinese children.

The Inn was full of war-orphaned children, almost 100; she must take them across the mountains and the mighty Yellow River to safety.

The next day they set out. Keeping away from the main trails they would avoid Japanese patrols. Gladys thought it would take 12 days to reach the Yellow River, but feared the millet they carried for food would not last that long. Most nights were spent in the open; by day they scrambled over rock slopes. They fell, they cried, they were hungry, their cloth-shod feet bled. Gladys sang hymns with them to keep them cheerful. When Japanese planes appeared, they scattered to hide. With feet blistered, sore and sun-cracked faces, they hobbled on and in 12 days saw the Yellow River.

But where were the boats to carry them across? Everything was deserted. Everyone had fled in fear of the Japanese. The older boys found some food in a deserted town nearby and then they settled down to wait for a boat.

Three days passed. They had nearly given up hope when, after kneeling to pray, rescue came – boats with Chinese soldiers, who ferried them across.

Before Gladys Aylward delivered her children to safety there were more mountains to cross, more nights spent on bare earth in rock shelters and in bitter cold. Yet whenever they neared despair, help always came. At last they reached the city of Fufeng, where the children were taken care of – and where Gladys collapsed with fever. Her doctor expected her to die. His only explanation for her recovery was that God had more work for her to do. She died in Taiwan in 1970, still preaching the Gospel and caring for orphaned Chinese children.

□ FIGHT FOR SURVIVAL □

Six million Jews died at the hands of the Nazis during the Holocaust of World War II. From this horror arose a passionate will to live, and to carry the ancient faith of Judaism into a new and better world.

The Nazis despised all religions, and after 1933 when Adolf Hitler ruled Germany, both Jews and Christians felt the cruel effects of this hatred. From 1935 anti-Jewish laws removed Jewish people's rights in Germany. For example, no Jew could be a teacher or a doctor. Over the doors of bakeries and dairies hung signs reading "Jews Not Admitted."

□ FIGHTING BACK IN POLAND □

Nesvizh is an ancient town, once in Poland, now within the Soviet Union. The town had a flourishing Jewish community, among them a young teacher named Shalom Cholawski.

When Poland collapsed under the Nazi invasion of 1939, Russian troops moved into the region around Nesvizh. The Communists were no friends to Judaism. Shalom and his friends smuggled religious books from house to house. The use of Hebrew and Yiddish was banned, and many Jews were arrested.

In 1941 Germany invaded Russia, and German armies raced eastward. The Russian troops fell back, leaving Nesvizh and other Polish towns to their fate.

The Germans ordered Jews to assemble in the main square. Those who were judged "useful" workers were shut up in a ghetto – a few tumble-down houses enclosed by barbed wire. The others were marched into the countryside and shot.

The Jews heard rumors of similar massacres in other towns. Shalom Cholawski was determined not to give up without a fight. "We must fight," cried Shalom. "We must defend the ghetto – as if we were the last Jews left on earth!"

When the police came to select more victims, no one flinched. "If some live, all shall live" was their resolve.

The Germans opened fire. The Jews' solitary machine gun (stolen from the Germans) was no match for their overwhelming firepower. Forced to give way they set fire to the houses. Small groups broke out of the ghetto, and ran for the forest, Shalom Cholawski among them.

The first Jewish ghetto uprising had taken place. Shalom escaped to join the Soviet partisans in the resistance to the German invaders. After the war he emigrated to Israel.

□ THE WARSAW UPRISING □

Warsaw, Poland's capital, had 400,000 Jewish citizens in 1940. By 1943 only 60,000 remained, walled up in the ghetto. Of the rest, most had died in Nazi extermination camps; others had succumbed to hunger and disease.

But the Nazis were not satisfied. Sixty thousand Jews were too many. In April 1943 the German army moved in to "clear" the ghetto – using tanks, artillery, and flame-throwers against pistols, rifles, and homemade grenades. The

Jews fought from every corner. When the Germans set fire to a building, its Jewish defenders often chose to die in the flames rather than surrender.

For a month the unequal battle raged. The Germans tried to flood the sewers and drive out the Jews with smoke bombs. At last on May 16 the German commander reported that the ghetto was no more; the Warsaw synagogue was blown up. Fewer than 4,000 Jews survived.

And yet there were still those who

Jewish defenders bravely meet the German attack in the Warsaw uprising.

sought to fight for their freedom. In August 1944 the war-ravaged city of Warsaw rose against the Germans. Among the 40,000 Poles who fought gallantly and hopelessly, Jews and Christians fought side by side. The uprising ended in October 1944; the last radio broadcast contained the words, "We are the conscience of the world."

☐ DEFYING HITLER ☐

A few Germans had the courage to stand up against the will of Adolf Hitler and the Nazis. Among them was Pastor Dietrich Bonhoeffer.

In April 1945 World War II was drawing toward its end. Among the many prisoners of the Nazis was a German Lutheran churchman named Dietrich Bonhoeffer. He had given an Easter sermon, speaking of hope in the resurrection of Jesus Christ. Suddenly, the door was flung open and armed guards entered to seize him.

Bonhoeffer was taken under guard to Flossenburg prison. A "trial" was held during the hours of darkness. At dawn, he and others accused of resisting Hitler's tyranny were hanged. It was April 9. Less than a month later Adolf Hitler was dead and the war in Europe was over.

Unity through faith

Dietrich Bonhoeffer was born in 1906 into a well-to-do family. He became a student of theology, as Germany struggled to recover from defeat in World War I. In 1933 Adolf Hitler became Chancellor. Many churchpeople sympathized with the Nazis and what they called the "moral rebirth" of Germany. But Bonhoeffer knew they were mistaken. The Nazi creed was immoral. He believed that Christians must oppose such an evil, and must unite across the world to do so.

Plotting against Hitler

Visiting his family in Berlin, Bonhoeffer

heard (from his brother-in-law) of secret plans to overthrow Hitler.

While on a lecture tour to America, friends asked him not to return to Germany. Bonhoeffer refused. He must share the horrors of Nazi rule with his fellow Christians. He would not fight for Germany, though he loved his country. If right were to triumph, he must pray for Hitler's defeat. In September 1939 World War II began.

A leader of the resistance to Hitler was Admiral Wilhelm Canaris, head of German military counter-intelligence. Under cover of working as an unofficial "spy"

for Canaris, Dietrich Bonhoeffer became a vital link between the resistance and the free world, using his church contacts. In 1942 he traveled to Sweden with secret peace proposals.

The Gestapo, however, was closing its net and in April 1943 Bonhoeffer was arrested. Such missions were very dangerous.

Prisoner of the Reich

Bonhoeffer was to remain a prisoner until his death. In July 1944 a rumor swept through his prison: Hitler had narrowly escaped a bomb meant to kill him. Hundreds of people had been arrested and cruelly executed. The Gestapo had old documents linking Bonhoeffer with Canaris and other conspirators. Barred from seeing his family and fiancée, he still hoped he might see peace one day.

Bonhoeffer's inner peace was a source of strength. A fellow prisoner remembered that "... he even won over his guards. He said to me over and over again that the only fight we lose is the one we give up."

Bonhoeffer continued his spiritual journey, and inspiration to those around him, until that April day in 1945 when the war was so nearly over. Then Hitler took his revenge. Bonhoeffer and others, including Canaris, were executed. The pastor went to the gallows bravely, kneeling to pray in the morning sunshine.

Dietrich Bonhoeffer was hurried by his guards into the gates of Flossenburg prison.

THE FIGHT GOES ON

Today, people still have to fight for their faith, for in many countries religious freedom is threatened by hostile governments. In others, religious leaders have led struggles to win justice and freedom for the poor and oppressed.

▫ THE BRAVE AFRICAN BISHOP ▫

The African country of Uganda is mainly Christian. In 1969 Janani Luwum became Anglican Bishop of Northern Uganda. Two years later the brutal Idi Amin seized control of the government. In 1972 Idi Amin ordered the expulsion of all Uganda's Asians — 80,000 people of Indian origin. Bishop Luwum protested. Next, terrible reports began to reach him of thousands of his fellow Africans murdered on Amin's orders.

In 1974 Luwum became Uganda's archbishop, and he worked with the Roman Catholic Cardinal Nsubuga to try to help the Ugandan people. Many priests had "disappeared," their bodies later found floating in the Nile River.

Amin drew up a "death-list," accusing Luwum of being in league with traitors. The archbishop calmly denied the charges as he stood before massed ranks of Amin's soldiers. Amin called him into a private conference room. The clergymen who had accompanied Luwum waited anxiously for his return, but the archbishop never reappeared. Later, the government radio announced that he had been arrested and had died in a "motor accident" while trying to escape.

Of course, this was not true. Luwum had been arrested and thrust into a death cell with other condemned men. He had prayed with them and for his captors. Then he was shot dead. Today, Amin's rule is over and the brave archbishop is remembered with pride.

▫ A PRISONER OF FAITH ▫

Richard Wurmbrand was born in Romania. An orphan, he was raised an atheist, but became a Christian. He began preaching to Russian prisoners of war during World War II. In 1945, when the war was over, Romania became a Communist state, and the Christian church was forced "underground." Wurmbrand and his fellow Christians met secretly, just as the first Christians met in the catacombs, underground. They worshiped in cellars and basements, in "safe houses," or in the woods.

Wurmbrand and his wife smuggled Bibles into Soviet barracks, talking about religion with men who, brought up in Communist Russia since the 1917 Revolution, had been told that all religion was superstition.

The underground church was in constant danger. One Sunday in 1948 Wurmbrand was arrested — dragged off the street and into a van by four men. For over eight years he simply vanished; his wife was told he was dead. In jail, Wurmbrand was tortured, beaten, and brainwashed to force him to give up his faith. He was refused books, and spent three years in solitary confinement.

In 1964, after a total of 14 years in prison with only one brief spell of liberty, Richard Wurmbrand was freed, after a "ransom" payment of money by Christians abroad. He left Romania, knowing that the work of the underground church would continue.

□ To Save El Salvador □

Oscar Romero was born in 1917 in a small town in El Salvador, Central America. He was apprenticed to a carpenter, but his ambition was to become a priest. This he did; he was ordained in Rome in 1942, and rose to become a bishop in 1970.

Bishop Romero did not seem destined for great deeds of bravery. In fact, some of his Salvadorean priests thought him too conservative and attached to the old ways. Seven out of ten people in the tiny republic were poor peasants; the country was controlled by a few rich families. The church had sympathized with the peasants but had done little, condemning revolutionaries as "communists." This had made some priests and nuns join the antigovernment parties.

In 1977 a new archbishop had to be chosen, and Romero seemed a safe choice. But the situation changed as violence in El Salvador became worse. Father Grande, a priest and a friend of Romero's, was shot dead by government troops after preaching antigovernment sermons. Romero rose to challenge the government in his friend's place. Fearlessly, he spoke out against all violence;

Richard Wurmbrand and his wife preach God's message to the Russian soldiers.

be it from the army, from right-wing terrorists, or left-wing revolutionaries.

His open support of the poor and downtrodden received the backing of Pope Paul VI in Rome. At home in El Salvador posters in the streets carried a brutal message: "Be patriotic; shoot a priest." Villages accused of "backing revolution" were attacked. Thousands of people disappeared. Romero used the radio to carry his message, and his broadcasts were listened to all over El Salvador.

Late in 1970 the army deposed the president and took control itself. The archbishop begged all sides to back away from civil war, before it was too late. In response, his radio station was blown up. He knew that his name was on the death list, but he refused to be silenced.

He called yet again for an end to repression and death. On March 24, 1980, he said Mass in the cathedral in San Salvador. Just as he finished his homily, he was shot. In the uproar, the killer escaped.

Thousands of country people flocked into the city for Romero's funeral; in yet one more horror, a bomb went off in the packed square before the cathedral; 40 people died in the panic.

There is still no peace in El Salvador, no end to the "madness" he saw, no sign of the "reason" he longed for. But Oscar Romero's name is now enshrined among the names of its national heroes.

□ THE PRIEST WHO DIED FOR POLAND □

On October 30, 1984, a body was found in a reservoir in Poland. It was that of a murder victim — a priest murdered not out of greed or from rage, but by government secret police. His name was Jerzy Popieluszko. His murder was front-page news in papers all over the world.

Father Popieluszko was, like most Poles, proudly patriotic. He was a supporter of the banned trade union Solidarity, whose members worked in the Warsaw steelworks and attended his church. A peasant's son, born in 1947, Father Jerzy had been ordained by Cardinal Stefan Wyszynski, a fearless critic of the Communist government.

Every month, Father Jerzy celebrated "masses for the homeland," and thousands came to hear him speak of what was wrong with Polish life, and with its Communist government. The government was not pleased, and Father Jerzy was threatened with arrest on charges of "slandering the state" and "poisoning" the minds of the people.

When the young priest left for a car journey to a nearby town, his friends expected him to return soon. When he did not, there was alarm. The discovery of Father Jerzy's dead body came as a national shock. He had been beaten up, bound, and brutally murdered. His killers were government secret police. They had thought, wrongly, that by killing him they could silence his arguments. But such was the widespread anger at the priest's death that they could not escape judgment. They were arrested and tried, and the government was forced to give a little more ground—another victory in the Polish people's fight for democracy and justice. Thousands came to Father Jerzy's funeral, to give thanks for the courage of this young priest whose death had shocked the nation and the world.

42

□ RELIGION IN CONFLICT □

Today, in many regions of the world people of sincere belief continue to fight for the faith they hold true. The most striking example is Iran under the leadership of the ayatollahs who preach an intense Islamic fundamentalism. In India, the Sikh nationalists' demand for a Sikh homeland is closely linked to religious conviction. In Tibet, the Chinese have tried since the 1950s to crush Buddhism, destroying monasteries and banning ancient religious practices. But Buddhism remains alive in Tibet, and has become one of the mainsprings for a Tibetan nationalist movement.

Religion has great power: to divide and to heal. It can cause tragedy – witness in particular the Middle East since the foundation of the Jewish state of Israel in 1948. Similarly, conflict between Hindus and Muslims led to the splitting of Britain's Indian Empire in 1947 into two independent countries: India (largely Hindu) and Pakistan (Muslim). More recently, in Lebanon, Christians and Muslims fight across street barricades. Religious differences have caused troubles in the Sudan in Africa, Indonesia, and Northern Ireland – where old fears and suspicions between Protestant and Catholic communities never seem to die.

A lack of tolerance for another person's religion can divide nations and damage hopes of peace. But religion can also be a great source of strength and healing. Christian leaders fight against apartheid in South Africa, while in Latin America priests working in the slums of the cities are fighting for their faith just as surely as did the missionaries of old.

Thousands of Poles mourned the death of Father Popieluszko, a brave and outspoken critic of the Communist regime in Poland.

⬜ COURAGEOUS FAITH FIGHTERS ⬜

Abu Bakr (573?-634) Follower of Muhammad, and first Muslim caliph: father of Muhammad's wife Aisha.

Alban, St. (d. about 304) First British martyr; converted to Christianity by a fugitive priest whom he sheltered and exchanged clothes with, to be martyred in the priest's place.

Ali (600?-661) Fourth Muslim caliph. Muhammad's son-in-law, and founder of the Shiite branch of Islam.

Alphege, St. (954-1012) Archbishop of Canterbury; captured by invading Danes when Canterbury was sacked in 1011, held ransom, then stoned to death at Greenwich.

Asbury, Francis (1745-1816) English Methodist who emigrated to America in 1771; recruited preachers on horseback, known as circuit riders, to bring the Gospel to the settlements.

Augustine, St. (d. 604) First archbishop of Canterbury, sent in 596 with 40 monks to reconvert the English by Pope Gregory I. Baptized Ethelbert, king of Kent, in 597.

Aylward, Gladys (1903-70) British missionary to China (later Chinese citizen), who led 100 children to safety over mountains during war with Japan.

Bonhoeffer, Dietrich (1906-45) German churchman who took part in resistance movement against Nazis. Imprisoned and executed.

Boniface, St. (about 675-754) Originally called Wynfrith or Winfrid, English missionary to Germany. Killed by pagan tribesmen.

Brainerd, David (1718-47) American missionary to the Indians of Massachusetts and New Jersey; died of tuberculosis.

Brébeuf, St. Jean de (1593-1649) French missionary to Canada, tortured and killed by Iroquois Indians.

Brown Blackwell, Antoinette-Louisa (1825-1921) American teacher and preacher, first woman minister of religion in the United States (1852). Campaigned for women's rights and abolition of slavery.

Campion, St. Edmund (1540-81) Jesuit priest and martyr sent in disguise to England to start a mission. Accused of plotting to murder Queen Elizabeth I, and executed at Tyburn.

Clare of Assisi, St. (about 1194-1253) Italian founder of the Poor Clares, following the rule of St. Francis. She insisted on a life of poverty and prayer for her nuns.

Clitherow, St. Margaret (1556-86) English martyr of York, a Protestant who became a Catholic. Imprisoned for not attending parish church, and later arrested again for sheltering a Catholic priest and attending Mass. Crushed to death.

Cranmer, Thomas (1489-1556) Archbishop of Canterbury, leader of Protestant reform in England. Supporter of Henry VIII, condemned for treason after accession of Mary I and burned at stake.

Crusaders Christian warriors who fought wars against Muslims for control of the Holy Land between 1095 and 1270.

Dalai Lama (b. 1935) High priest of Tibetan Buddhism, thought by followers to be a god. Escaped in 1959 during Chinese occupation of Tibet and now lives in India. Tibetans continue to resist Chinese attempts to destroy their religion.

Eliot, John (1604-90) English-born missionary in America, translated the Bible into Indian dialect. Worked near Boston, Massachusetts, setting up Indian missions.

Fisher, St. John (1469-1535) Bishop and martyr, beheaded for not accepting King Henry VIII as head of the Church of England.

Fox, George (1624-91) Founder of the Society of Friends. He once told a magistrate to "tremble (quake) at the word of the Lord" earning his followers the nickname Quakers. Many Quakers were jailed for refusing to swear oaths, even in court, and for refusing to fight in wars.

Francis of Assisi, St. (1182-1226) Founder of the Franciscan order. Taken prisoner during a war in Italy; later renounced his inheritance for simple clothes and life to travel as a pilgrim and preach. Met the Sultan when trying to convert Saracens in the Holy Land.

Frumentius, St. (d. about 380) Founder of the Abyssinian Church. Taken as a slave to Abyssinia (Ethiopia) after shipwreck, gained king's favor and preached Christianity throughout kingdom.

Grenfell, Sir Wilfred (1865-1940) British medical missionary, worked in Labrador and Newfoundland for 40 years.

Guyard, Marie (1599-1672) French missionary to Canada, who founded a convent in Quebec and stayed on despite threats from hostile Indians during Iroquois wars in 1648.

Hennepin, Louis (1626?-1705?) Belgian missionary and explorer who journeyed among Iroquois and other Indian tribes; explored with La Salle, captured and held by Sioux Indians for several months.

Hussites followers of **John Huss (1370-1415)** Bohemian religious reformer who was burned at the stake as a heretic.

Joan, St. (1412-31) Young French peasant girl whose "voices" urged her to save France from foreign rule. Captured and burned to death; made a saint in 1919.

Judson, Adoniram (1788-1850) American Baptist missionary to India and Burma, 1813. Translated Bible into Burmese.

King, Martin Luther, Jr. (1929-68) American Baptist minister and leader of civil rights movement. Awarded the Nobel peace prize in 1964, was assassinated the same year.

Knights Hospitaler Religious and military order of knights at the time of the Crusades. Later based on the island of Rhodes, and fought Turks. Today based in Italy, and involved in medical relief work.

Knights Templar Founded by Hugues de Payncs of Burgundy in 1119 to defend Jerusalem against Muslims. Withdrew to Cyprus and were suppressed on the Pope's orders in 1312. The last Templar leader was burned at the stake in Paris.

Kolbe, Maximilian, St. (1894-1941) Polish priest, missionary to India and Japan. Arrested during World War II by Nazis and sent to Auschwitz concentration camp, where he volunteered to die instead of a fellow prisoner.

Las Casas, Bartolomé de (1474-1566) Spanish missionary in West Indies and Mexico, fought for rights of native Americans who were being enslaved by Spanish colonists.

Latimer, Hugh (1485?-1555) English champion of Reformation, arrested during reign of

A Knight Hospitaler

Christian Crusaders capture Acre in the Holy Land.

Queen Mary and burned at stake; he advised his fellow sufferer Ridley by saying, "Be of good comfort, Master Ridley, and play the man; we shall this day light such a candle by God's grace in England as I trust shall never be put out."

Livingstone, David (1813-73) Scottish missionary and explorer in Africa, from 1841 until his death. Exposed evils of slave trade to the outside world.

Loyola, Ignatius St. (1491-1556) Spanish soldier and founder of the Jesuits (Society of Jesus), which devoted itself to missionary work and to countering the Protestant Reformation.

Lull, Ramon (1235?-1315) Spanish missionary; studied Arabic and went to North Africa to preach to Muslims; stoned to death.

Luther, Martin (1483-1546) German Protestant reformer, whose quarrel with the Catholic church symbolized the split known as the Reformation.

Luwum, Janani (1922-72) Ugandan archbishop who was put to death for standing up to the tyrannical dictator Idi Amin.

Lwanga, Charles and companions, **Martyrs of Uganda (1885-86)**, group of 22 Africans; one named Joseph Mkasa reproached King Mwanga for the murder of missionary James Hannington. Charles Lwanga was in charge of the king's pages and had baptized some. The Christian martyrs were burned alive inside reed mats.

Maccabees (about 168 B.C.) Jewish family who revolted against attempts to make Jews follow Greek religion.

Martel, Charles (689?-741) Frankish warrior ruler who defeated Muslim attempts to invade southern France in 732. Grandfather of Charlemagne.

Martin, St. (about 330-397) Bishop of Tours, missionary and founder of monasteries. Roman soldier who renounced war after being converted to Christianity. When charged with cowardice, offered to stand in front of battle line armed only with the sign of the cross.

Massacre of St. Bartholomew 1572 Terrible slaughter of Huguenots (French Protestants) in Paris.

Miki, Paul (d. 1597) Christian martyr in Japan; a Jesuit priest, he and 25 other Christians were crucified during the persecutions of Hideyoshi.

Mindszenty, Jozsef (1892-1975) Hungarian church leader who defied the Communist government and was jailed, 1949-56. Later spent 15 years in refuge within U.S. Embassy in Hungary.

More, Sir Thomas, St. (1478-1535) Lord Chancellor of England, 1529; refused to take oath affirming King Henry VIII as head of church in England. Executed for treason. Canonized 1935. Wrote *Utopia*, describing an ideal state.

Morrison, Robert (1782-1834) Scottish missionary who was the first Protestant missionary to China.

Muhammad (570?-632) Founder of Islam, born in Mecca in Saudi Arabia. Called on people to worship the one true God and abandon their old pagan ways.

Niemoller, Martin (1892-1984) German Lutheran pastor, who led church opposition to Nazis in 1930s; for which he was imprisoned.

Patrick, St. (389?-?461) Born in Britain, captured by Irish pirates when 16, and sold as a slave. Escaped after six years in Gaul, returned to Britain. Called in a dream to preach to Irish; founded churches and converted Ireland.

Patteson, John Coleridge (1827-71) English missionary in Melanesia, killed by natives.

Paul, St. (about A.D. 3-67) Born a Jew, converted to Christianity on road to Damascus. Became missionary to Gentiles and made three great journeys, founding many churches to which he sent letters (epistles). Story told in Acts of the Apostles in Bible. Believed to have been tried and executed in Rome.

Peter, St. (d. 64) Disciple of Jesus Christ, preached in Jerusalem, imprisoned by Herod Agrippa but escaped. Tradition says he went to Rome and died a martyr during persecutions of emperor Nero.

Popieluszko, Jerzy (1947-84) Polish priest who was murdered by police for his antigovernment preaching.

Ricci, Matteo (1552-1610) Italian Jesuit missionary to India and China; founded mission in Peking.

Ridley, Nicholas (1500?-1555) English reformer and martyr, bishop of Rochester and of London. Helped Cranmer to compile English prayer book. Declared a heretic when Mary I became queen, and burned at stake.

Stoning of St. Stephen, first Christian martyr.

Romero, Oscar (1917-80) Archbishop of El Salvador, murdered because he criticized the government and terrorist "death squads."

Saladin (1138-93) Full name Salah-al-din Yusuf Ibn-Ayyub, leader of Muslims against Crusader army of Richard I of England (Third Crusade).

Scharansky, Anatoly (b. 1948) Soviet Jewish dissident who spent nine years in jails and labor camps before being freed in 1986, whereupon he emigrated to Israel.

Sebastian, St. (d. 288) Soldier serving Roman emperor Diocletian. He made many Christian converts. Said to have been executed for disobeying emperor's command not to preach.

Slessor, Mary (1848-1915) Scottish missionary, who left job in factory to spend most of her life working in the Calabar region of Nigeria.

Stephen, St. (d. about A.D. 36) First Christian martyr, stoned to death after being accused of blasphemy.

Victims of the Holocaust Six million Jews who were tortured and executed by the Nazis during World War II.

Williams, John (1796-1839) English missionary, explored the South Seas, converted Samoan islanders. Killed and eaten by natives of Erromanga in the New Hebrides.

Willibrord, St. (658-739) English missionary to Friesland and Denmark, assisted in his work as "Apostle to the Frisians" by St. Boniface.

Whitman, Marcus (1802-47) American missionary doctor, who with his wife Narcissa (1808-47) helped open up Oregon for settlement. Killed by Cayuse Indians during unrest following a measles outbreak brought by settlers.

Wyszynski, Stefan (1901-81) Polish cardinal, opposed Nazis during World War II: imprisoned by Communists 1953-56, and later worked for peace and reconciliation in Poland.

□ INDEX □